T0150417

not a guide to
Edinburgh

**Bruce Durie
with Carolyn Becket**

The
History
Press

First published in 2012

The History Press
The Mill, Brimscombe Port
Stroud, Gloucestershire, GL5 2QG
www.thehistorypress.co.uk

British Library Cataloguing in Publication Data.
A catalogue record for this book is available from the British Library.

ISBN 978 0 7524 7148 8

Typesetting and origination by The History Press
Printed in Great Britain

The Edinburgh Coat Of Arms

The city's coat of arms has had various incarnations. From at least the fourteenth century, the Royal Burgh of Edinburgh used armorial seals and so on, but it was only in 1732 that arms were formally granted by the Lord Lyon, Scotland's heraldic authority. These were used by Edinburgh Town Council until Scottish local government was reorganised in May 1975, and the successor, City of Edinburgh District Council, had a new coat of arms (followed by another in 1996 for the new City of Edinburgh Council).

*

They're all much the same, featuring the castle on its hill, an anchor as the crest (signifying the title of Admiral of the Forth, held by the Lord Provost) and the motto: *Nisi Dominus Frustra*, 'except the Lord in vain', associated with the town since 1647 and taken from Psalm 127:1: 'Except the Lord keep the city, the watchman waketh but in vain'.

*

The supporters are a doe – for St Giles, the city's patron saint – and a woman, perhaps a reference to an older name, *Castrum Puellarum* (Castle of the Maidens, as it housed a nunnery and was a safe haven for royal females).

Contents

Edinburgh's Past

'Dunedin', 'Edina', 'the Athens of the North', 'Auld Reekie' – Edinburgh has a lot of names, some historical and some fanciful inventions at the time of the Enlightenment of the mid-1700s.

Initially a hill-fort on a volcanic crag-and-tail, the old Din Eidyn went from being the fastness of the kingdom of the British Gododdin to a Scots-dominated stronghold about AD 950. It became a town in its own right (separate from the fort) between Malcolm II taking the Lothians from Northumbria (1018) and David I granting land to the Church of the Holy Rood (1124). When William the Lion confirmed David's charter in 1170 he used the Latinised name *Edenesburch*.

One of the earliest Royal Burghs (but not yet the capital – that was Dunfermline), Edinburgh quickly grew in the late medieval and Renaissance periods to become the economic, cultural and political centre, and the focus for the religious tussles of the Reformation in the mid-1500s and the wars in the next century.

The Parliament remained in Edinburgh in 1603 when James VI took over the English throne as James I; this went away in 1707 at the Union and came back in a new guise at Devolution in 1999, with a controversial building that significantly over-ran its cost estimates.

Three Towns (or Four)

The Old Town was constrained by the old Flodden Wall, so it grew vertically, with some High Street buildings four or five storeys at the front and twice as many or more down the back, with warren-like closes betwixt and between.

The New Town was a Georgian exercise planned as the very antithesis of the cramped tenements of the Royal Mile – a grid of wide streets, high ceilings, airy rooms, and lots of windows.

The Victorian era saw the growth of Princes Street's shops opposite the now-drained open sewer that was the Nor Loch with its brand-new railway line and lovely gardens. There was also growth in solid working-class districts like Slateford, Polwarth and Gorgie, cheek by jowl with well-to-do mansions in Corstorphine, the Grange, Morningside and elsewhere. These houses are now worth a fortune but expensive to heat and maintain, leading to a whole tier of the upper-middle classes being asset-rich but cash-poor or, as they say locally:

> 'Pianos and kippers,
> Fur coat and nae knickers'

During this time, Glasgow outgrew its old rival in population and industry, becoming the Second City of Empire – but Edinburgh retained its cool as the capital.

The twentieth century was typified by bungalows straggling along the main roads out of the city, and social housing in what became Pilton, Wester Hailes, Muirhouse, Craigmillar and elsewhere.

Cultural Orientation

On chips – Salt'n'vinegar (not salt'n'sauce, which is considered a Glasgow aberration).

Jenners – The most famous department store.

Tartan Tat – To the bewilderment (but commercial delight) of the natives, almost the whole of one end of Princes Street and all of the Royal Mile are occupied by seemingly identical emporia purveying an eclectic mix of 'authentic' Highland wear, 'Clan' keyrings, tiny bagpipes and toffee made from hairy cows.

'Getting off at Haymarket' – Local euphemism for *coitus interruptus*.

Sex – What coal comes in.

Trams – Oh, don't mention the trams!

Ice-cream and cafés – There is a considerable Italian population, which imported a fine tradition of restaurants, fish-and-ship shops, cafés and Hokey-Pokey (ice-cream).

The Festival – Be **very** careful here, as 'The Festival' refers to the official Edinburgh International Festival, as opposed to its far larger and much more popular offspring, The Fringe, and the dozen or so other festivals that run at the same time. Try getting a hotel room in August!

How, Where, What?

How big is it?

Depends what you mean. Edinburgh has swallowed up previously separate burghs and towns like Canongate, Leith, Portobello, Joppa and Cramond and now occupies more than 100 square miles. The centre is compact, and almost all visitor activity is concentrated in the Old Town, New Town and Leith Shore.

Where it is?

55°57′11″N 3°11′20″W

OS grid reference: NT275735

Time zone: UTC/GMT (UTC+1) in summer

What is it?

Scotland is a sovereign nation within the United Kingdom, and Queen Elizabeth II is separately Queen of Scots and Queen of England, just as she is separately Queen of Canada, Australia, the Bahamas and lots more places.

The Unitary Authority has been the City of Edinburgh Council since 1996 but city status was granted in 1889.

The old county of Midlothian (previously Edinburgh-shire) no longer exists except in the imagination of the Post Office and as a Lieutenancy.

There is a small part of Nova Scotia at Edinburgh Castle. In an early cash-for-honours scheme and to encourage the settlement of 'New Scotland', which lies between New England and Newfoundland, James VI and I created the Baronetage of Nova Scotia in 1624.

Because anyone granted land had to 'take sasine' by symbolically receiving earth and stone, but Nova Scotia was a bit far away, it was decided to make a part of the Castle Esplanade legally part of Nova Scotia. This plaque commemorates the grant to Sir William Alexander in 1621.

NEAR THIS SPOT IN 1625
SIR WILLIAM ALEXANDER OF MENSTRIE
EARL OF STIRLING, RECEIVED SASINE
OR LAWFUL POSSESSION OF THE ROYAL
PROVINCE OF NOVA SCOTIA BY THE
ANCIENT AND SYMBOLIC CEREMONY OF
DELIVERY OF EARTH AND STONE FROM
CASTLEHILL BY A REPRESENTATIVE OF THE KING
HERE ALSO (1625–1637) THE SCOTTISH BARONETS OF NOVA
SCOTIA RECEIVED SASINE OF THEIR DISTANT BARONIES
PRESENTED BY THE PROVINCE OF NOVA SCOTIA

Geotopography

There aren't many places in the world with two socking great volcanos in the middle. Edinburgh is built around a basalt plug with its glacier-formed tail down the Royal Mile, and has gradually surrounded Arthur's Seat and Salisbury Crags in Holyrood Park. Some denizens include other products of vulcanism and erosion (Calton Hill, Corstorphine Hill, Blackford Hill, the Braid Hills) to make the mythical seven that every city seems to claim – except, possibly, Amsterdam.

The city and its suburbs are physically bounded by the Pentland Hills to the south and the Firth of Forth to the north, and is fringed by a green belt about 2 miles wide from Prestongrange to Dalmeny. This was intended to prevent urban sprawl and the swallowing-up of small settlements – but that didn't stop (for example) Edinburgh Airport.

Edinburgh has no equivalent of Glasgow's urban motorway, except a short stretch at the West End known as the Hyperspace Bypass. There is no subway system, but the city centre is now hostage to a multi-billion pound tram system to replace the one they threw away fifty years ago because buses were better.

The tram will eventually go to Edinburgh airport, which is just as well – despite two main train lines going right past the end of the runway, there's no train station there. A needlessly complicated and expensive rail-link scheme – with special trains, interlinks, tunnel and an underground station – was passed and then quietly dropped in 2007.

Distance From...

Place	Miles	Km
Athens, Greece	1,757	2,827
Brussels, Belgium	471	757
Campbell Island, NZ (the furthest away place you can actually get to)	12,070	19,420
Sydney, Australia	10,480	16,865
Centre of the Earth	3,976	6,399
Dublin, Ireland	216	348
London, England	398	644
Glasgow, Scotland	52	84

Other places called...

Edinburgh, South Australia

Edinburgh, Indiana, USA

Edinburgh Island, Nunavut, Canada

Edinburgh, Maryland, USA

New Edinburgh, Nova Scotia

Edinburgh, North Carolina, USA

New Edinburgh, Ontario

Edinburgh, Ohio, USA

Edinburgh, Limpopo

Edinburgh, South Carolina, USA

Edinburgh, North West SA

Edinburgh, Zimbabwe, USA

Edinburgh, Northern Cape, SA

Edinburgh of the Seven Seas

Edinburgh, Texas

Edinburgh, South Australia

Edinburgh, Indiana, USA

Edinburgh Island, Nunavut, Canada

Edinburgh, Maryland, USA

New Edinburgh, Nova Scotia

Edinburgh, North Carolina, USA

New Edinburgh, Ontario

Edinburgh, Ohio, USA

Edinburgh, Limpopo

Edinburgh, South Carolina, USA

Edinburgh, North West SA

Edinburgh, Zimbabwe, USA

Edinburgh, Northern Cape, SA

Edinburgh of the Seven Seas

Edinburgh, Texas

Edinburgh's Place in the World
Edinburgh is on more or less the same latitude as Jutland, the Alaska Peninsula, Quebec and Moscow.

Edinburgh is due south of Orkney and its line of longitude also passes though Caerphilly, France, Spain, the Gulf of Valencia, Algeria, Mali, Burkina Faso, Togo, Ghana, and the Atlantic Ocean on its way to Queen Maud Land in Antarctica (claimed by Norway).

Twin Towns

Town twinning started after the Second World War to foster mutual understanding between cities and countries, initially in Europe.

Edinburgh is twinned with:

Aalborg, Denmark (1991)

Dunedin, New Zealand (1974)

Florence, Italy (1964)

Kiev, Ukraine (1989)

Krakow, Poland (1995) – 'Partner City'

Kyoto, Japan (1994) – 'Friendship Link'

Munich, Germany (1954)

Nice, France (1958)

San Diego, California, USA (1977)

Santa Cruz de la Sierra, Bolivia (1996)

Vancouver, Canada (1977)

Xi'an, Shaanxi province, China (1985)

Facts and Figures

Population (2009): 486,120

Male population: 235,249

Female population: 250,871

Households: 218,774

Births (11.3 per 1,000): 5,502

Deaths (10.3 per 1,000): 4,266

Natural change: 1,236

Population growth (-0.54 per cent): 2,625

Net migration (-4.1 per 1,000): 5,066

Literacy: 99 per cent

Population density per square km: 1,811

Life Expectancy at Birth
Female: 80.1 years

Male: 75.3 years

Ethnicity
White Scottish: 71 per cent

Other white British: 12 per cent

White Irish: 1 per cent

Other white: 10 per cent

African: 1 per cent

Chinese: 0.8 per cent

Indian: 1.6 per cent

Other: 2 per cent

(Source: General Register Office for Scotland)

Historical Demography

Edinburgh is the second largest city in Scotland after Glasgow and the seventh largest in Britain. The Larger Urban Zone surrounding the city covers 665 square miles, with a population of 778,000.

Is Edinburgh getting smaller or bigger – and if so, why? In 2001, 22 per cent of the population was born outside Scotland (12.1 per cent in England). But since 2004 there has been considerable migration from new accession states, such as Poland, Lithuania and Latvia.

This is now slowing, and it is no longer the case that the city is overrun by Australians working in the bars.

Foreign Nationals Aged 16+

Origin	2005	2009
European Union	6,830	5,710
Asia/Middle East	1,450	2,350
Americas	780	800
Australia/New Zealand	1,230	790
Africa	570	590
Rest of Europe	190	190
Total	11,060	10,430

(*Source: Department of Work and Pensions*)

Street Names

Princes' Street would have been St Giles' Street but George III thought it was too similar to a London slum area of that name, so the City Fathers made reference to the Royal Princes, the Duke of Rothesay (who became George IV) and the Duke of York. James Craig, who planned the New Town, would have called it South Street.

George Street was also so named to cheer up George III. Much the same applied to Hanover Street and Frederick Street, George IV Bridge, Regent Road – and so on.

George Square, on the other hand, was named by the architect James Brown after his elder brother, George.

Queen Street is for Charlotte of Mecklenburg-Strelilz, George III's queen.

St Andrew Square and **St George's Square** (which became Charlotte Square), at either end of the New Town, were named to reflect the union of Scotland and England, as were the two smaller parallel roads, Thistle Street and Rose Street.

Antigua Street, like Jamaica Street, was named for economically important islands in the West Indies in around 1800.

Picardy Place was originally 'Little Picardy', after the Huguenot refugees who fled Picardy in 1685, mainly weavers of silk and cambric (from Cambrai). Sadly, the silkworms and mulberry trees didn't take to the Edinburgh climate.

Pilrig derives from Pilrig House, so named for a fifteenth-century Peel Tower on a ridge (rig). Owned originally by Patrick Monypenny, and possibly the country house of Mary of Guelders, it was later with the Balfours, R.L. Stevenson's mother's family. The young RLS was sent there to the 'country' when his chest was bad.

Duddingston village is named not from the Gaelic for 'sunny side of the hill', as is often claimed, but comes from the Doden family, who settled there in eleventh century and made it Dodinstoun.

Lawnmarket was the place to buy and sell 'lawn' (fine linen).

The Pleasance is either a reference to a 'pleasant' place to take the air, or from the convent of St Mary of Placentia.

Potterrow was at one time a 'village' of pottery workers.

Historical Timeline

According to a chronicle at Iona, Edinburgh was overwhelmed by an unknown invader, but probably Oswald of Northumbria.

Queen (later Saint) Margaret dies at the castle and her chapel is built.

Roman forts at Cramond and Inveresk.

The first St Giles' Kirk is said to have been built, but no one knows for sure.

Malcolm II makes Edinburgh fully part of Scotland.

Castle recaptured by Thomas Randolph, 1st Earl of Moray.

*c.*200   638   854   1020   1093   1314

*c.*580   *c.*840   *c.*960   1074   *c.*1125   1296

Cinaed mac Ailpin (Kenneth MacAlpine) raids the Lothians as part forging the united kingdom of Alba (Scotland).

Indulf and his Scots take Edinburgh.

Edward I takes and re-fortifies Edinburgh.

Military campaign under king Mynyddawc Mwynvawr, as told in Welsh poem *Y Gododdin* (southern Scotland was British and spoke a language like Welsh.)

Malcolm III starts rebuilding the castle.

First documented evidence of a church in the 'burgh of Edin', and David I grants burgh status, founding Holyrood Abbey in 1128.

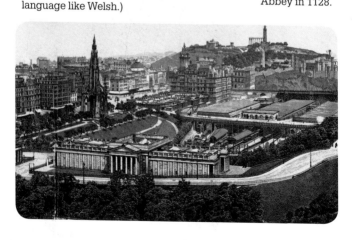

The treaty to ensure an independent Scotland is signed.

Edinburgh's rebuilt castle is the royal residence – the burgh has 4,000 dwellings.

Edinburgh acknowledged as the capital.

Edinburgh Castle is flattened by David II.

Robert II grants land for the Tolbooth.

The defensive wall is completed.

1328 1330 1360 1386 1437 1450

1329 1334 1364 1387 1440 1457

When the English take Berwick, Edinburgh grows in importance.

St Giles' gets five new chapels after English depredations and becomes the High Kirk.

'Mons Meg' (a 20-inch siege cannon) arrives at the castle.

Robert Bruce confirms burgh status and creates a port at Leith.

David II gives the ground for a new tron (weighing place), starts fortifying the castle, and promptly dies there.

Edinburgh has half of the Scottish wool trade and the Cordiners (shoemakers) are an incorporated guild.

Edinburgh is home to one of the three Supreme Courts of Scotland.

Scots beaten at Flodden, so a new defensive south wall is built.

The Earl of Hertford burns the town, the palace and the abbey, and the English come back in 1547 to do it all again.

Stone-built tenements start to appear.

James V decides to show the world who is boss, so he enters Edinburgh with an army and has Holyrood Palace built.

The Flodden Wall is finished and Edinburgh has a population of some 12,000, with almost 400 craftsmen and as many merchants.

1458 1485 1513 1528 1544 1559

1474 1507 1520 1530 1558 1559

More craft guilds are incorporated. 1477: The High Street becomes the site for all fifteen of Edinburgh's markets.

James IV grants a patent for the first printing press to Chapman and Myllar.

There are almost 300 alewives (brewers), one for every forty inhabitants.

John Knox is minister at St Giles' church

There are riots over French persecution of Protestants.

The rivalry between the Douglases and the Hamiltons leads to a running battle in the High Street and the Earl of Angus (a Douglas) takes the city.

1560

The Reformation starts in earnest as English and French troops pull back.

1565

Mary, Queen of Scots, marries Henry Stuart (Lord Darnley) assassinated in 1567.

1566

Mary captive in Holyrood Palace and her favourite, David Rizzio, is murdered.

1569

Plague in the city.

1573

The Regent, the Earl of Moray, takes back the castle for a pro-Mary faction and starts fortifying the Half-Moon Battery.

1579

James VI arrives for his state entry.

1582

The University of Edinburgh is given its royal charter as the fourth university in Scotland.

1592

The first Edinburgh census is taken – there are some 8,000 adults.

1593

The Earl of Bothwell tries to take the city.

The Reformed Church demands to be armed against Catholics.

1596

1603

The Scottish Post Office is headquartered in Edinburgh and King James VI gets a set of golf clubs.

1604

Execution by hanging of the Laird of MacGregor and fourteen others for the Colquhoun massacre.

Plague (again!).

Rioters protest about the new Prayer Book and the bishops being on the privy council.

Kirk built in Canongate.

The city is ordered to clean up its streets and the population hits 25,000.

Scottish coronation of Charles I at St Giles' – but he annoys the Presbyterians by giving Edinburgh a bishop.

The town buys the area around the West Port and the Marquis of Huntly is killed by covenanters.

1619   1624   1633   1637   1649   1650s

1610   1621   1632   1636   1640   1650

Edinburgh and Leith are Scotland's main ports.

The new Parliament House is started.

Parliament House finished.

Printer Andrew Hart publishes Napier's book of Logarithms and much else besides.

Tron Church building starts; population now about 30,000.

James Graham, 1st Marquess of Montrose, hanged, and Edinburgh Castle surrenders to Oliver Cromwell. James Colquhoun builds his first fire engines as the Palace of Holyrood is destroyed by fire.

First newspaper
in Scotland
published
by Thomas
Sydserf.

Advocates'
Library
founded
(now NLS).

Jacobites
attack castle,
but fail.

Stagecoach
service to
Glasgow.

Fire leads to
new stone
buildings;
population now
around 60,000.

eneral
ssembly of the
irk stopped by
ie English.

Slaughterhouse
moved from
Grassmarket.

1653   1661   1670s   1678   1682   1700   1715

1652   1660   1670   1677   1681   1690s   1707

oach service
o London
egins (a two-
eek journey).

Water pipes
laid from
Comiston
Springs.

Royal College
of Physicians
founded.

Act of
Union of
Parliaments
proclaimed.

Committee of
Estates formed to
govern Scotland.

First coffee
house opens.

Professional classes
(lawyers, doctors etc.)
outnumber merchants.

35

Golf is played on Bruntsfield links and the Royal Burgess Golfing Society founded.

Bonnie Prince Charlie arrives in the city.

Stagecoache to Newcastle (seven days)

First circulating library starts and the medical school launched.

The Scots Magazine is published and Edinburgh has four printing businesses.

Playhouse Theatre opened in Canongate.

Daniel Defoe visits.

1718   1720s   1722   1726   1729   1735   1737   1739   1744   1745   1746   1747   1751   1758

Signet Library founded.

Lord Provost removed following riots.

Old Town considered run down; new public buildings, roads and bridges proposed.

The British Linen Co. founded.

Edinburgh Evening Courant first published.

First infirmary is opened.

Earliest recorded rules of golf drawn up and played at Leith Links.

Penny Post
begins service.

The Edinburgh Review
starts publication.

South Bridge
completed.

James
Craig wins
competition
to design the
New Town.

Eight legal
distilleries in
Edinburgh
(but 400
illegal).

Charlotte Square
completed and
the National
Museum of
Antiquities
founded.

Coal gas
made
available.

1766   1773   1777   1788   1800   1802   1817

1763   1771   1775   1781   1788   1801   1802

Sir Walter
Scott born.

The Mound
is opened
to traffic.

Earthquake:
no damage
except to a
barn.

Bank of
Scotland
builds head
office.

Construction of
North Bridge by
Robert Adam
(completed in
1772).

Directory of
prostitutes
and brothels
published.

William (Deacon) Brodie
executed; building of
Old College begins.

Union Canal is started; Calton Hill observatory is built.

Cholera ravages the city; *The Scotsman* newspaper absorbs *The Caledonian Mercury*.

Edinburgh to Glasgow railway opens.

Fire destroys buildings.

Burke (of Burke and Hare) hanged.

New Town finished; Old Town is now no more than a slum.

Scott Monument completed; North British Railway founded.

1818   1824   1829   1832   1835   1842   1846

1822   1826   1831   1833   1836   1843   1850

George IV visits Edinburgh and wears a kilt over pink tights. First Highland and Agricultural Show.

Royal Scottish Academy founded.

The Innocent Railway to Dalkeith opens.

Leith dock construction bankrupts the city.

William Playfair's Royal Institution opens.

Disruption, and the Free Church of Scotland forms.

Scottish National Gallery founded.

British Linen Bank opens new headquarters at St Andrew Square.

National Gallery opens.

Flying Scotsman express passenger train service to London – journey takes ten and a half hours.

New Royal Infirmary and School of Arts/ Watt Institute (later Heriot-Watt) completed.

Moray House starts teacher training.

Free public library opens.

Building of Edinburgh College of Art starts building.

1851   1859   1862   1879   1890   1905   1907

1856   1861   1865   1889   1902   1906   1910

Canongate burgh joins Edinburgh.

Report condemns sanitation in Edinburgh.

Earthquake hits Edinburgh (again!).

King's Theatre built at Tollcross.

Industrial museum (now the Royal Museum of Scotland) opens; one o'clock gun established to help ships in Leith set their clocks.

Waverley Station and North British Hotel (now The Balmoral) completed.

First electric trams.

Leith incorporated
into Edinburgh.

BBC Scotland
headquarters open.

Empire Palace
Theatre burns
down, killing
nine people
plus 'the Great
Lafayette',
whose ghost is
said to haunt
the building.

National
Library of
Scotland
founded, based
on the former
Advocates'
Library.

Debutantes
received by
Queen for the
last time.

Ring roads
and bypass
planned.

Princes Street
railway station
closes.

1911   1920   1925   1932   1949   1958   1965
1911   1923   1928   1947   1956   1959   1966

Last cable-
pulled tram.

First Edinburgh
International
Festival.

Old Town
population
down to 2,000.

Palladium
and La Scala
Cinemas open;
Empire Palace
reopens; Usher
Hall built.

The Mound gets
'electric blanket' under
road.
Flying Scotsman runs non-stop to
London; Broughton Street gets road
traffic lights, the second in the UK.

Heriot-Watt
becomes a
university.

Old Town restoration and re-population.

The new Museum of Scotland built.

Finally, trams get the (partial) go-ahead.

Commonwealth Games; James' Centre and New Andrew's House open.

Edinburgh Castle Scotland's leading paid tourist attraction. Holyrood is eighth.

Scottish Parliament Building opens.

1970   1980   1990   1998   2004   2011
1975   1986   1996   1999   2009   2012

Edinburgh disappears into Lothian Regional Council but absorbs South Queensferry and Kirkliston.

Common-wealth Games (again!).

City of Edinburgh Council created.

Scottish Parliament opened by the Queen.

Homecoming Scotland and Clan and Family Gathering held.

The Forth Bridge painting stops and the bridge itself is awarded a Gold *Blue Peter* Badge.

Craigmillar Castle

Craigmillar Castle is one of the best-preserved medieval castles in Scotland, famous as the place where Mary, Queen of Scots recovered after the birth of her son, the future James VI and I, and where the plot was hatched to murder her husband Henry Stuart, Lord Darnley.

By the mid twentieth century, Craigmillar had become a by-word for depressed urban living. But in the 1970s, Craigmillar found itself leading a grass-roots development of artistic outpouring that led to the Craigmillar Festival, Theatre Workshop Edinburgh, Communiversity, Arts As The Catalyst, a Neighbourhood Workers Scheme and a Creative Shared Government vision.

It started in 1962, when Peffermill Primary School Mothers Club felt frustrated at the lack of response to requests for music, drama and art lessons. They went door-to-door, assembling local talent and putting on a People's Festival. Mixed in with the fun was political action, and culture became tinged with satire as community-composed musicals and historical productions addressed the area's issues of deprivation and social problems.

Official recognition and charitable status came in 1970, and 6 years later, the Craigmillar Festival Society had 600 workers and 1,500 volunteers, with an attendance in 1976 of some 17,000 people. An anti-poverty research grant from the EU helped. Helen Crummy, one of the originators, was awarded an MBE in 1973 and later an Honorary Doctorate.

In many ways, Craigmillar was the inspiration for the Notting Hill Carnival and a number of the local performers went on to have professional careers – notably Micky MacPherson, whose Plum Films won a BAFTA for their first short film, *Tumshie McFadgen's Bid for Ultimate Bliss*.

Mysteries and Ghosts

The Ghostly Piper and the Underground City

Workmen discovered a tunnel at the castle and a piper offered to march along it playing while others tracked the sound down the Royal Mile. At the Tron the music stopped. The piper was never seen again, and the tunnel was sealed – but when everything is quiet, his bagpipes can still be heard. Mind you, it's hard to walk down the Mile without hearing the faint sound of the pipes…

Likewise, many vaults, wynds and passages under South Bridge were built over (but can still be visited) and among the many ghost stories is the 2003 radio recording on which an ethereal voice was heard shouting 'go away' (in Gaelic).

Charlotte Square

Go and listen for the sound of a ghostly piano, look for the hooded eighteenth-century figure and try to avoid the spectral horse and carriage that runs when the traffic is absent.

Greyfriars Churchyard and Bluidy Mackenzie's Head

A modern and well-documented haunting concerns George Mackenzie of Rosehaugh, Lord Advocate to Charles II and known as 'Bluidy Mackenzie' for his persecution of the Covenanters. When he died in 1691 he was entombed close to where many of his victims had been held. In December 1998, a homeless man broke into Mackenzie's mausoleum for shelter, opened the coffin for some reason and was surprised by the skeleton leaping out at him. He didn't stay long.

Then in 1999 weird events started happening – visitors have been attacked by an invisible assailant, other have reported feeling ill and finding scratch-marks on them the next day and several have been knocked senseless.

In 2004, two teenagers were arrested for breaking into the Black Mausoleum, playing football with Mackenzie's skull and using it like a glove puppet.

The many fires around the area where Mackenzie lived, including the Radisson Hotel in 1992, are credited to his poltergeist.

Many pubs and closes claim a ghost, especially those from the old coaching days, such as the White Horse.

Whistlebinkies
This pub in Niddry Street (where Bluidy Mackenzie lived) has an 'imp' who slams doors, stops clocks and breaks things; it also has a long-haired man in seventeenth-century clothes called 'The Watcher'.

The Playhouse Theatre
This theatre is haunted by a spectre called Albert, said to be a stagehand who died in an accident or killed himself.

Jamaica Street
This pub had many reports around 1800 of a man in a large red hat, and one James Campbell was accused by his landlord of spreading ghost stories to get his rent down. He was fined £5 and told not to speak of it again.

The Scotsman Hotel
is the site of the old newspaper offices and has a few ghosts, including 'the phantom printer'.

St Mary's Street
In 1916 a woman was viciously murdered here. She is occasionally seen standing in the road, covered in blood and looking totally dazed.

Balcarres Street
This street is haunted by 'the Green Lady', thought to be one Elizabeth Pittendale, who was caught canoodling with her stepson and murdered by her husband who found them at it.

Leith Corn Exchange
This pub has the ghost of an earlier publican who hanged himself after accusations of torturing children. His appearance is said to have been captured by an American television crew filming there.

GREYFRIARS

IN GREYFRIARS CHURCH THE NATIONAL COVENANT WAS ADOPTED AND SIGNED 28TH FEBRUARY 1638. IN THE CHURCHYARD ARE OBJECTS OF HISTORICAL INTEREST SUCH AS THE MARTYRS' MONUMENT TOWARDS THE NORTH EAST AND THE COVENANTERS' PRISON TOWARDS THE SOUTH WEST ALSO THE GRAVES OF MANY SCOTSMEN AND CITIZENS OF EDINBURGH OF WHOM SOME OF THE MOST IMPORTANT ARE:-

JAMES DOUGLAS	EARL OF MORTON REGENT OF SCOTLAND	DIED	1581
GEORGE BUCHANAN	HISTORIAN AND REFORMER	"	1582
ALEXANDER HENDERSON	CHURCHMAN AND STATESMAN	"	1646
SIR GEORGE MCKENZIE	KING'S ADVOCATE	"	1691
MARY ERSKINE	SCHOOL FOUNDER	"	1707
WILLIAM CARSTAIRS	STATESMAN	"	1715
GEORGE WATSON	SCHOOL FOUNDER	"	1723
COLIN MACLAURIN	MATHEMATICIAN	"	1746
WILLIAM ADAM	ARCHITECT	"	1748
THOMAS RUDDIMAN	GRAMMARIAN	"	1757
ALLAN RAMSAY	POET	"	1758
WILLIAM ROBERTSON D.D.	HISTORIAN	"	1793
JAMES HUTTON	GEOLOGIST	"	1797
DUNCAN BAN MACINTYRE	GAELIC POET	"	1812
WILLIAM CREECH	BOOKSELLER	"	1815
JOHN KAY	CARICATURIST	"	1826
HENRY MACKENZIE	"THE MAN OF FEELING"	"	1831
THOMAS MCCRIE	HISTORIAN	"	1835
WILLIAM MCGONAGALL	POET	"	1902

The Museum of Childhood

Well worth a visit, it is also said that visitors to this museum can hear the cries of mothers and children from a nursery sealed up after a plague, with the victims still inside.

Queensberry House

A true story – at Queensberry House, while the Duke was out pacifying the crowds in the run-up to the unpopular Union of 1707, his mentally-defective son, the Earl of Drumlanrig, escaped from his usual confinement and was found roasting and eating alive a kitchen boy. His screams can still be heard in the room – now the office where MSPs claim their expenses!

No. 5 Rothesay Place

Here, the householders bought some used furniture in the 1950s belonging to a sailor who had recently died. Ever after they were pestered by a twelve-inch-high figure they came to call 'Gnomey'.

No. 15 Learmonth Gardens

Never take a bone from an Egyptian mummy's tomb, as the owners of 15 Learmonth Gardens did in the 1930s – the house was beset by the ghost of an Egyptian priest, accompanied by noises and objects being flung about.

Mary King's Close

For a really creepy experience, visit this close. In the seventeenth century this was a bustling, thriving area at the heart of Edinburgh, and Mary King was a prominent local business-woman. So how, 400 years later, did her Close and its neighbouring wynds and vennels find itself intentionally buried underground? Visit and find out the historical and archaeological stories behind the myth!

Edinburgh's Climate

Edinburghers moan about the weather – mainly the winds – but the temperate maritime climate is surprisingly mild considering the city shares a latitude with Newfoundland and Moscow. Winter daytime temperatures rarely go below freezing. On the other hand, any temperature above 75°F (23°C) is considered 'a scorcher'. However, the position between hills and coast funnel the prevailing warm south-west wind from the North Atlantic Current that drops most of its rain on Glasgow but still howls through Edinburgh at times from October to May. Easterly winds are drier and colder, often bringing a particularly penetrating coastal fog known as 'haar' or 'Scotch Mist'.

The local joke is 'if you don't like the weather, wait 20 minutes', but there is some justification for this: at times the weather of four seasons – sunshine, biting wind, drizzly rain and a snowstorm – have been recorded in the time it takes to walk along Princes Street.

Any snowfall (which usually lies for about a day) brings all traffic and railways to a halt and the newspapers herald the end of civilisation.

A Day in the Life

0650 – First train arrives at Waverley Station from Glasgow Queen Street.

0716 – First sleeper arrives from London.

0800 – Grab a copy of *The List* and a Festivals guide (there is ALWAYS some festival or other on) and plan your day.

0805 – Have a full Scottish breakfast at one of the many outdoor cafés in the Grassmarket (if the weather permits – indoors if not) then take a gentle saunter round the many wee bookshops up the West Port.

0930 – Get active. Climb Arthur's Seat and have an unparalleled vista over the city, or stroll round the Chinese Hillside at the Botanic Gardens or explore Dean Village or Hermitage.

1130 – Culture time. Head for the Museum of Modern Art near the West End, or the Scottish National Portrait Gallery at the East end of Queen Street.

1230 – Shopping! Princes Street is traditional, but George Street is far better. Grab lunch.

1300 – Make sure you're close enough to the castle to hear the one o'clock gun go off. It has recently been quietened.

1330 – History is all around. Start at Castle Hill with the Camera Obscura and walk down the Royal Mile to Holyrood, checking out all the vennels and closes as you go.

1530 – Quality time in Canongate Churchyard, the Museum of Childhood, the People's Story, Holyrood Palace or Dynamic Earth.

1700 – Thirsty? Lots of great pubs on the way, but try the historic Tollbooth Tavern or head off to the baroque Café Royal or Inspector Rebus's favourite, the Oxford Bar in Young Street.

1800 – Dinner time. Edinburgh is not short of great restaurants, but head for Leith where you'll find the Michelin-starred eateries Kitchin, Martin Wishart and The Plumed Horse plus a great selection of less stratospheric dining places.

1930 – Take one of the ghost tours or a guided visit to the ultra-creepy Mary King's Close.

2100 – There is bound to be some festival or other on, but otherwise check out Bedlam Theatre (Edinburgh University), the Stand Comedy Club or numerous other late venues.

2300 – Club it! The Bongo Club puts on an array of club nights from reggae and hip hop to R&B, soul and funk, hard rock and even ceilidh. Then there's the burlesque-gothic Voodoo Rooms. If you fancy a quieter time, go for live traditional music at many bars including the Royal Oak, folkies' favourite Sandy Bell's or Whistlebinkies.

2330 – Last train leaves for Glasgow (or you could get the 2333 and wait at Falkirk Grahamston for five and a half hours).

2340 – Last sleeper leaves for London Euston.

A Free Day Out

Sit in Princes Street Gardens, admire the view of the castle and decide whether Stevenson based *Treasure Island* on the gardens' shape.

Check out the recreation of sculptor Eduardo Paolozzi's studio, at the Dean Gallery.

Visit the Dean Cemetery and walk along the Water of Leith.

St Giles' and both cathedrals called St Mary's have marvellous architecture.

Walk along the beach at Portobello or out to Cramond Island.

Have your picture taken beside Greyfriars Bobby or (more imaginatively) Robert Fergusson at Canongate Kirk.

Go to the roof terrace at the National Museum.

Tour the Scottish Parliament building and see the MSPs in action (booking essential, yawning forbidden!).

Walk over Arthur's Seat to Duddingston.

Browse the second-hand shops in Stockbridge.

Book a free 'taster session' at the National Records of Scotland and look up your ancestors.

Peruse the Scottish Poetry Library.

Go up to the Castle Esplanade and watch the sun setting over the Pentland Hills,

Sit in the 'Secret Garden', Dunbar's Close (if you can find it).

Edinburgh Vistas

Edinburgh in Numbers

The average price of a house in Edinburgh is £220,000 (40 per cent above the rest of Scotland) and a two-bed flat will cost between £525 a month in Gorgie and almost £900 in the New Town. Almost two thirds of Edinburgh's dwellings are flats.

Edinburgh is ranked first in the UK for 'quality of life', and eighth in the world.

About a third of the workforce lives outside the city. Over half travel less than 3 miles to work. Over 60 per cent of adults use a bus service at least once a week, and 25 per cent every day.

One in five residents walks to work.

The annual traffic volume is about 1,900 million vehicle miles, 200 million on urban motorways.

Edinburgh's railway stations serve 23 million passengers each year – 20 million at Waverley alone.

Edinburgh has almost as many air passengers as Luton or Birmingham (about 9 million annually, but now falling).

Gross Disposable Household Income is the second-highest in the UK.

Recorded crime has dropped by a third in the last decade.

Edinburgh is second only to London in Gross Value Added per employee. The largest employment sectors are business services and finance (about 50 per cent), followed by the public and voluntary sectors (25 per cent).

Three of the hundred largest FTSE 100 and four Fortune 500 companies are based in Edinburgh, more than any other UK city except London.

The highest employers are, in order: City of Edinburgh Council, NHS Scotland, Edinburgh University, Lloyds Bank, Royal Bank of Scotland, Standard Life, Scottish Government, police, AEGON UK and Scottish Widows. Strange as it may seem for such a tourist capital, only about 27,000 (8 per cent) of workers are in accommodation or food service.

There are over 3.5 million tourists visit every year, occupying nearly 13 million bednights and spending over £1 billion. Most come from England (42 per cent), followed by France (16 per cent) and America (6 per cent).

About 1.2 million visitors go to the castle each year.

Edinburgh is the most ethnically mixed place in Scotland, second for non-white inhabitants (4 per cent) and third for non-Scottish whites (17 per cent).

Catch a Festival

When are they and how many attend?

Puppet & Animation Festival (March/April): 2,311

Ceilidh Culture (March/April): 24,409

Science Festival (April): 198,979

Beltane Fire Festival (30 April): 11,000

Imaginate Festival (May): 11,100

Film Festival (June): 44,456

Royal Highland Show (June): 187,600

Magic Festival (July): 2,500

Art Festival (July to September): 669,000

Jazz and Blues Festival (August): 37,300

Edinburgh Mela (August): 34,590

Military Tattoo (August): 222,000

Fringe (August): 2,870,724

Spirituality and Peace Festival (August): 25,000

Festivals' Cavalcade (early August): 100,000

International Festival (August/Sept): 396,716

Book Festival (August): 315,555

Politics Festival (August): 52,750

International Marketing (late-August): 10,000

Interactive Festival (late-August): 324, 025

Television Festival (August): 2,000

Storytelling Festival (October): 15,124

Hogmanay (30 December): 250,000

(Dates may change annually)

An Edinburgh Glossary

Scots may or may not be a separate language, depending on who you believe – although the records of Parliament up to 1707 were written in Scots. Gaelic is a minority sport in Scotland, spoken by as few as 50,000 people. There are more native Urdu speakers. But at least everyone can agree that each region of Scotland has its own 'patter'. Here are some examples of the Edinburgh's *lingua franca*.

Blether – Chat or gossip, but without necessarily talking 'havers' or 'mince'.

Baltic – Rather chilly for the season.

Buckfast commando – Intoxicated, aggressive and intrepid individual.

Cheesing – Pleased, smiling as if to a camera.

Cream puff – Bad mood or pout.

Doosh – Deal a blow to, especially with the fist.

Foostie – Mouldering, bad-smelling or old.

Gorgie Kiss – Approximation of one's forehead to the nose of an interlocutor (aka 'nut cutlet').

Gutted – Disconsolate beyond all telling.

Havers – Conversation devoid of informational value (similar to Mince).

Heidjin – Person in authority, outranked by a 'High Heidjin'.

Jump – Launch a surprise attack on someone, usually from hiding, at night, and in number.

Minging – That which 'mings' (odoriferous).

Nash – Move quickly, when avoiding pursuit.

Nat King Cole – Sexual congress (same as 'Cameron Toll').

NID – Variant of NED (Non-Educated Delinquent) but in particular a denizen of Niddry.

Nip (someone's) heid – Irritate and annoy.

Nippy – Sarcastic and back-talking.

Pish – Rather disappointing.

Poppy – Negotiable currency.

Pure – Term of emphasis, as in 'pure dead brilliant!'

Radge – Angry and unstable beyond reason.

Radgecase – A person so inflicted.

Radio Rental – Of unstable mind.

Rank – Of unpleasant aspect or odour.

Scoobied – Unaware, confused, clueless ('I hivnae got a Scoobie-Doo').

Scoop – Partake of alcoholic beverage.

Shahoorsur! – untranslatable

Soap-dodger – Of inadequate personal hygiene, and suspected of being Glaswegian.

Spraff – Talk continuously, particularly when helping police with enquiries about another.

Swedge – Altercation involving fisticuffs.

Weegee – Contraction from 'Glaswegian', associated with 'Soap-dodger'.

Edinburgh on the Page

'With regard to the buildings that have of late risen in this City with such incredible rapidity, we may venture to say, that, in regularity and magnificence, they are scarcely equalled, or at least not excelled, by any in Europe.'
Robert Heron, *Scotland Delineated*, **1790s**

'When God Himself takes to panorama painting, it turns out to be strangely beautiful... I have found the beginning of my Scottish Symphony there today.'
Felix Mendelssohn, 1829

'Nature... has laid every foundation, and disposed of every line of its rocks and its hills, as if she had designed it for the display of architecture.'
Edinburgh Review, **1838**

'Who indeed that has once seen Edinburgh, but must see it again in dreams waking or sleeping?'
Charlotte Bronte, 1850

'This generous and magnificent city... so distinguished in literature and the arts... coming back to Edinburgh is to me like coming home.'
Charles Dickens, after a reading of A Christmas Carol at the Music Hall, 1858

'The most beautiful town in the world.'
Benjamin Disraeli, writing to John Murray from the Royal Hotel, 1825

'There is no street in Europe more spectacular than Princes Street; it is absolutely operatic.'
Henry James, after a visit in 1878

'It seems like a city built on precipices, a perilous city. Great roads rush down hill like rivers in spate. Great buildings rush up like rockets.'
G.K. Chesterton, *London Illustrated News,* **1905**

Glasgow is null,
Its suburbs shadows
And the Clyde a cloud.
Dundee is dust
And Aberdeen a shell.
But Edinburgh is a mad god's dream,
Fitful and dark…
C.M. Grieve (before he became Hugh MacDiarmid), 'Midnight' in *Northern Numbers,* **second series, 1921**

'The most beautiful of all the capitals of Europe.'
John Betjeman, *First and Last Loves,* **1952**

'Nature took trouble over the site of Edinburgh'
William Power, *The Face of Edinburgh,* **1939**

'A setting for an opera nobody performs nowadays, an opera called Scottish History.'
Alasdair Gray, *Janine,* **1982**

Famous for...

Style – The Old and New Towns have UNESCO World Heritage Site status.

Words – The world's first UNESCO City of Literature, with a rich literary past and present.

Urbanism – European City of the Year, 2006, praised as an 'attractive, safe and enticing place for people to play, visit and enjoy'.

Education – The excellent universities, medical and veterinary schools, the Art School and education generally.

'Best City' – Winner of more than thirteen UK Awards.

A Good Night Out – Voted best in an Amstel/Virgin Radio poll, for 'the rich diversity and vibrancy of its venues'.

Living in – More leisure facilities and services per head than any other regional city in Britain.

Festivals – 3.1 million visitors a year can't be wrong. Edinburgh's Festivals contribute over £184 million annually to the Scottish economy, and 100 million people watch the Military Tattoo every year on television.

Visiting – Five of Scotland's top ten visitor attractions are in Edinburgh. Famous former visitors abound: in Greyfriar's graveyard, Charles Dickens saw a stone saying 'Uriah Heep, Meal Merchant' and turned it into 'Mean Merchant' – hence the character in his novel *David Copperfield*.

Infamous For...

The more-or-less warm welcome – Edinburgh is allegedly where you will hear, 'You'll have had your tea' (whether you have or not).

The tram system – It may or may not be a good idea eventually, but the construction has caused years of traffic mayhem and lost revenue to local shops and businesses.

Unreliable weather – Forecasts more than a day in advance are considered science-fiction.

Presbyterian attitude – 'You're not here to enjoy yourself!' (Even though you are.)

The hills – Almost everywhere you'll want to go is uphill from where you are, and in the older parts of town not everywhere has wheelchair access.

Beggars – How can such a rich city have so many homeless people? There is a plan to have vouchers exchangeable for food and clothing, instead of money to fund drug habits.

Parliament building – The original estimate spiralled from £40 million to £109 million, and it actually cost £431 million. At least it was finished, though, unlike…

'Edinburgh's Disgrace' – The 1822 Calton Hill Acropolis, which ran out of money early on.

Buildings and Architecture

With over 4,500 listed buildings and forty conservation areas covering a quarter of the city there is no shortage of stunning architecture.

Old Town
The **Royal Mile** is in fact five streets (Castle Esplanade, Castlehill, Lawnmarket, High Street, Canongate and Abbey Strand) and just over a mile long from castle to palace.

Other Buildings to Check Out Are:
The former **Tolbooth Highland Church**, now The Hub, headquarters of the Festival Society.

The **Assembly Hall of the Church of Scotland** and **New College** (both best appreciated from the other side).

Gladstone's Land, a seventeenth-century townhouse.

The baroque **Bank of Scotland** headquarters

Parliament Square, now home to the Court of Session (Scotland's highest civil court), **St Giles' High Kirk** and the **Mercat Cross** from which royal proclamations are read.

After **Moubray House** (oldest inhabited dwelling in Edinburgh) and the so-called **John Knox's House** (should be Abbot George Durie's House!) is the **Netherbow**, once a fortified gateway in the Flodden Wall, now home to Netherbow Theatre and the Scottish Storytelling Centre.

The **World's End Pub** marks the old boundary of the burgh with Canongate, which was controlled by Holyrood Abbey.

The Tolbooth houses **The People's Story** (social history museum) and a decent pub.

Canongate Kirk has a terrific graveyard.

New Town

Much Palladian architecture from the Georgian period, but the most outstanding are:

St Andrew Square at the eastern end, with the Royal Bank of Scotland building and **Charlotte Square** to the west end, with **Bute House** and other Adam buildings.

Between these, check out the various banks which have been turned in to pubs and restaurants.

Princes Street is home to the grandiose mid-1800s **National Gallery** and **Royal Scottish Academy**, which compete for attention with the **Scott Monument**.

New Build

The **Scottish Parliament Building** and **Dynamic Earth** are modern counterparts to the Palace of Holyroodhouse and the ruins of Holyrood Abbey.

Museums

The best free museums and galleries are:

City Art Centre
Six exhibition galleries, home of 3,500 works of Scottish art and a leading exhibition venue.

Fruitmarket Gallery
Across Market Street, this non-profit arts space has exhibitions, commissions and education.

Stills Gallery
Contemporary photography, plus a programme of talks and photographic amenities.

Writer's Museum (Lady Stair's House)
Dedicated to Burns, Stevenson and Scott, it has manuscripts, artefacts and portraits relevant to the three, and the house is great in itself.

Museum of Childhood
The first in the world when it opened in 1955, with toys, songs, games and memorabilia.

Museum of Edinburgh
Displays reflect Edinburgh's story from the prehistoric to now – the 1638 National Covenant, Greyfriars Bobby's actual feeding bowl, and a great collection of silver and glass.

People's Story
Social, oral and pictorial history of those working and living in Edinburgh, with sights, sounds and smells, a prison cell, a 1940s kitchen and more.

Royal Museum of Scotland
The biggie – a world-class assembly of science and technology, archaeology, natural history and decorative arts, the Victorian building was extended in the 1990s with a roof-terrace café.

National Gallery Complex
Three interconnected buildings host Scotland's best fine art collections and major international exhibitions. The Weston Link has eats, drinks and shops. Take a free bus to…

Gallery Of Modern Art and Dean Gallery
Cubism, Scottish Colourists, Magritte, Dada, Paolozzi sculptures and lots more to see.

Scottish National Portrait Gallery
Impressive building with portraits of Scotland's movers and shakers, refurbished in 2011.

Edinburgh's Green Spaces

Princes Street Gardens

Formed from the Nor Loch – originally defensive as well as a place to drown witches – when the site became silted, marshy and foetid, it was drained in the eighteenth century to provide gardens for the New Town residents and later a path for the railway. Every Christmas the eastern part hosts a winter market. The western part, with its outdoor theatre and the Ross Fountain, is the major site for Hogmanay. The ruin of the old wellhouse (1362) is accessible across bridges and paths.

Calton Hill

Smallest of Edinburgh's seven hills (Arthur's Seat, Braid Hills, Blackford, Corstorphine, Castle Hill and Craiglockhart), Calton has great vistas of the city centre and the Forth. The Nelson Monument (1822) was built in memory of those who died in the Napoleonic wars. The National Monument was supposed to be a Parthenon, but funds ran out after the base and columns were erected. The original Observatory (1792, by James Craig, architect of the New Town) was replaced in 1818 with a building by William Playfair, who also designed the nearby Dugald Stewart monument.

The Meadows

South of the university, this grassed area is where the locals walk, cycle and play ball games. It had been the Burgh Loch, a source of water for drinking, brewing and clothes washing. By 1871 it was just a rubbish tip. The Free Meadows Festival is in June and some Edinburgh Festival events are held there.

Dean Village

The Water of Leith carves a picturesque valley through this lovely residential area with a history steeped in mill-working. The new Anthony Gormley statues complement the 1833 bridge by Thomas Telford.

Duddingston Village

A lovely church, super views, nice loch with a bird sanctuary and the oldest pub in Edinburgh – how many more reasons do you need to visit this ancient weaving village? Also visit Dr Neil's Garden and the original Skating House.

Currie and Balerno

At one time separate, these villages nestle at the foot of the Pentland Hills with great walks all the way back to Leith, or into the Pentlands themselves.

Edinburgh's Seaside

Cramond

The Romans camped here, where the River Almond reaches the estuary. Be charmed by the white cottages, tea rooms, beach and – if the tide is out – the causeway to Cramond Island with its Second World War shelters.

Leith

A separate burgh (and proud of it) since 1833, Edinburgh's port was rejoined with the city in 1920, against almost everyone's wishes. The decline of shipping and industry of the twentieth century was halted in the 1990s, producing a pulsating residential and leisure area full of cafés, bars, restaurants and the Royal Yacht *Britannia* plus the Ocean Terminal shopping mall and cinema.

Portobello and Joppa

Edinburgh's Blackpool, Portobello has a wonderful sandy beach and a promenade with cafés, pubs, restaurants, swimming pool and Turkish baths, although the funfairs, pier, open-air pool, donkey-rides and most amusement arcades are long gone thanks to cheap foreign package holidays. Joppa, Portobello's upmarket-ish neighbour, is fiercely independent.

Scientists, Inventors and Doctors

Really too many to mention, but…

John Napier, inventor of logarithms

Joseph Black, pioneer of thermodynamics

Medical researchers **Joseph Lister** (antisepsis) and **James Young Simpson** (anaesthetics)

Daniel Rutherford, who first isolated nitrogen

James Clerk Maxwell, founder of the modern theory of electromagnetism

Alexander Graham Bell, teacher of the deaf and telephone pioneer

Charles Darwin, who studied here before discovering natural selection

James Hutton, 'Father of Geology'

Ian Wilmut, who cloned Dolly the sheep, now stuffed and on display at the National Museum of Scotland (the sheep, that is…)

Peter Higgs, who proposed the Higgs Boson

Elsie Inglis, doctor and Suffragist campaigner

Sophia Jex-Blake, Edinburgh Medical School's first female student (except for the one who dressed as a man all her life), and now commemorated by a plaque there

James Nasmyth, inventor of the steam hammer

Robert Knox, anatomist (of Burke and Hare fame)

D'Arcy Wentworth Thomson, mathematician and zoologist

Facts About Edinburgh Authors: Robert Louis Stevenson

He was christened Robert Lewis Balfour Stevenson and Frenchified his middle name.

A sickly child, his mother mother kept him indoors during the damp Scottish winters and his nurse read to him from the history of Scotland and the Bible.

He was sent, for his health, to Balfour relatives living at Pilrig House, 'in the country' – in fact, it's in Pilrig Park about half-way down Leith Walk, and, after being derelict for a time, is now luxury self-catering apartments.

Robert Louis Stevenson was destined to be a lighthouse engineer like his father Thomas, grandfather Robert and uncles Alan and David, but he preferred books and history, so he studied law instead.

He took a train all the way across America to California to persuade the much older Fanny Van de Grift Osbourne to marry him. She already had a husband and children. On the way, he met many emigrant Scots heading East – returning home again. The journey nearly killed him.

While living in Westbourne, Dorset, he named his house Skerryvore after the tallest lighthouse in Scotland, built by his uncle Alan.

In 1890, Stevenson bought 400 acres on the island of Upolu, Samoa, and named his estate 'Vailima'. The islanders called him 'Tusitala' ('Teller of Tales') and he became very friendly with the King of Hawaii, David Kalakaua.

He wrote the first draft of his most famous work, *The Strange Case of Dr Jekyll and Mr. Hyde*, in three days in 1885, but after he let his wife read it, he burned the manuscript then wrote the whole novella again from scratch in another few days.

When he died in Samoa, his death certificate was signed by the local doctor, B. Funk.

Facts About Edinburgh Authors: J.K. Rowling

Joanne Rowling is not a native Edinburgher, but was born in Yate, near Bristol, just south of a town called Dursley. The name famously became a surname in her books.

She is known as 'JK' because the publisher of the first novel felt male readers would be biased against a book written by a woman – but as she had no middle name, she added K after her favourite grandmother, Kathleen.

The seven *Harry Potter* books have sold over 450 million copies worldwide, and Stephen King has reviewed them all for the *New York Times Review of Books*.

She writes all of her books in longhand, rather than on a computer, and became the first billionaire author (according to *Forbes* magazine).

A friend reports: 'She signed a copy of the second Harry Potter book for me with a dedication to my three children. In their haste to read it, one of them took it in the bath, dropped it and destroyed the book and the inscription.' That may be a common story!'

J.K. Rowling was one of at least three Edinburgh authors (along with Alexander McCall Smith and Ian Rankin) who once lived in that part of Morningside known as 'Writer's Block'.

Nicolson's Café on Nicolson Street was where she went as a single mum, as the staff there let her write for long periods over one coffee with her daughter asleep in a buggy. There was a plaque outside but it kept getting stolen. The Elephant House Café on George IV Bridge makes a similar claim to fame and is more or less a shrine to the author.

Although there is no connection between Hogwarts and the gothic Fettes College, the famous Edinburgh boarding school has cashed in mercilessly on the similarities – even running potion-making courses in the chemistry lab and the chance to handle live owls.

Musicians and Bands

Edinburgh has produced many fine popular musicians, such as the **Bay City Rollers** (1970s pop favourites), **Edwyn Collins** (who had a solo hit with 'Girl Like You' in 1994) and **Shirley Manson** (lead singer with Garbage).

But perhaps the greatest unsung hero is **Len Partridge**. Len taught Bert Jansch, co-wrote 'Hey Joe' with Yankee Bill Roberts in an Edinburgh coffee bar in 1957, and he influenced a generation of musicians. Most of this came about during an extraordinarily creative period in Edinburgh – late 1959 to early 1962 – and in an extraordinary place. The Howff at No. 369 High Street was possibly Britain's first real folk club. Founded by the enigmatic Roy Guest (possibly hiding from creditors in London) and his girlfriend, Jill Doyle, it brought together Len Partridge (the local blues hero), Archie Fisher (who gave guitar lessons there), Bert Jansch (who lived in a series of squats with Robin Williamson and Clive Palmer, instigators of The Incredible String Band) Owen Hand (guitarist and musicographer), Hamish Imlach (who taught John Martyn) and Jill Doyle's half-brother Davey Graham (whose deceptively simple composition 'Angi' became the must-play tune for every aspiring guitarist thereafter).

Visiting American talent included Pete Seeger, Sonny Terry and Brownie McGhee. The Howff became a tea-room and is now a lawyer's office, of all things!

Architects

William Adam (1689-1748), Royal Infirmary

James Adam (1732-1794), son of the above Adam. Designed many buildings in Glasow

John Adam (1721-1792), Milton House

Robert Adam (1728-1792), Charlotte Square

Robert Rowand Anderson (1834-1921), Scottish National Portrait Gallery

Hippolyte Blanc (1844-1917), Christ Church, Morningside

David Bryce (1803-1876), Scottish Baronial country houses

William Burn (1789-1870), many Scottish churches

James Craig (1739-1795), Edinburgh New Town

James Gillespie Graham (1776-1855), Hopetoun House.

Thomas Hamilton (1784-1858), Royal High School and Scottish Political Martyrs' Monument

John Lessels (1809-1883), The Walker Estate

David MacGibbon (1831-1902), Royal Bank of Scotland

John Mylne (1611-1667), Heriot's Hospital

John Dick Peddie (1824-1891), Cockburn Street

John More Dick Peddie (1853-1921), Longmore Hospital

William Henry Playfair (1790-1857), National Gallery of Scotland and the Royal Scottish Academy

Benjamin Marcus Priteca (1889-1971), Theatre architect

Witold Rybczynski (1943-), widely respected for his books and articles on architecture

James Smith (1645-1731), refurbished Holyrood Abbey, designed Caroline Park and Canongate Kirk

William Weir (1865-1950), castles nationally

Artists and Sculptors

You possibly couldn't find two Edinburgh artists who make for a greater contrast than portraitist **Sir Henry Raeburn** (1756-1823) and artist-sculptor **Eduardo Paolozzi** (1924-2005), who must have been conceived on the 100th anniversary of Raeburn's death.

Founder of the 'Scottish School' of painting, Raeburn was born in Stockbridge, lost his father early, was raised by his brother and was educated at Heriot's, then a free school for orphans and the children of distressed gentlefolk. He started painting miniature portraits but the leading Edinburgh painter, David Martin, encouraged him to paint in oils. Raeburn married a wealthy widow in 1778 and started to acquire and develop property, making a fortune in the process. Joshua Reynolds advised two years study in Italy, and after his return Raeburn's George Street studio became the portraiture centre for Edinburgh society. He became a member of the Royal Academy in 1815, was knighted when George IV visited Scotland in 1822 and was appointed His Majesty's Limner for Scotland, dying shortly after in 1823.

Eduardo Paolozzi was born in Leith to Italian parents, studied at Edinburgh's College of Art, St Martin's in London and the Slade, Oxford. In Paris from 1947 to 1949, he met the leading lights of surrealism and 'art brut'. Originally sculpting robot-like epitomes of the machine age, he moved to prefabricated aluminium and brass casts. Paolozzi also produced graphic art and ceramics, made films and wrote, taught textile design in London until 1955, designed Tottenham Court Road tube station in London with its coloured mosaics, and spent many years teaching in Germany. His library and studio have been recreated at the Dean Gallery, Edinburgh.

Facts About Edinburgh Actors: Alastair Sim

Alastair Sim CBE is best known for his definitive 1951 Scrooge in *Oliver Twist* and as the criminally-inclined Fritton brother-and-sister twin roles in the *St Trinians'* films. But here are a few lesser-known factoids:

Born 9 October 1900, he was christened Alastair George Bell Sim.

The youngest of four children, he initially worked in his father's tailor's shop in Lothian Road. He then sold ties at up-market outfitters Gieves & Hawkes.

Educated at Heriot's School, he studied to be an analytical chemist, joined the Officer's Training Corps just before the end of the war in 1918 and worked on the land for a year in the Highlands, living rough.

After studying at Moray House teacher training college, he was Fulton Lecturer in Elocution at Edinburgh University from 1925 to 1930, mainly teaching ministers-in-training how to articulate.

He returned to Edinburgh as rector from 1948 until 1951 – entitling his inaugural address 'The Qualified Fool' – and received an honorary LLD.

During the Second World War he and his wife, Naomi, moved out of London and took in evacuees – one was George Cole, who arrived when fifteen and stayed until he was twenty-seven, becoming more like a son to them.

Awarded the CBE in 1953, he later refused a knighthood.

When he died, Sim left his body for anatomy.

In 2008 English Heritage erected a blue plaque to Alastair Sim at 8 Frognal Gardens, London, NW3.

Hearts v. Hibs

Edinburgh has two professional football clubs: **Heart of Midlothian** (Hearts) and **Hibernian** (Hibs).

While not as overtly sectarian as the Rangers-Celtic divide in Glasgow, both teams have obvious religious affiliations. Hearts fans are known as Jambos (a reference to 'Jam Tarts' and the plum-coloured strip) and Huns (Hanoverian, i.e., Protestant) and the livery of Hibs is green and white, reflecting their origins with Irish immigrants and explaining the nickname 'Cabbages'.

These teams have the longest rivalry of any two clubs in the world, as the Edinburgh Derby (any game in which they play each other) has been going since their first match in The Meadows in 1875. There, Hearts played the first 20 minutes with only eight men. So far, the score in Derbys is:

Hearts 136 wins, Hibs 85, draws 88 in 309 competitive matches.

Hearts 140, Hibs 112, in some 300 'friendlies' and other games.

Hibs claim to have achieved the best scoreline (7-0 at Hearts' home ground, Tynecastle, in 1973) and so do Hearts (10-2 in an 1893 friendly, and 8-3 in a league match in 1935).

The record attendance for any Edinburgh Derby match was 65,860 on 2 January 1950 (Hearts won 2-1 at Hibs' ground Easter Road), which is also the largest crowd at any Scottish football match not played in Glasgow.

Otherwise Famous

Tony Blair, British Prime Minister from 1997 to 2007

Archibald Cleghorn (1835-1910), married into the royal family of Hawaii

Elaine Davidson, Guinness World Record holder for 'Most Pierced Woman'

Tom Farmer, who started Kwik-Fit in 1971

William Burke and **William Hare**, serial killers. Famous for body-snatching, they are now memorialised in a lap-dancing establishment, one of three at Edinburgh's 'Pubic Triangle'.

Field Marshal Sir Douglas Haig, 1st Earl Haig

George Heriot ('Jinglin' Geordie'), goldsmith and philanthropist

John Knox, Protestant reformer

David Murray, ex-chairman of Glasgow Rangers, set up Murray International Metals in 1974

John Porteous, city guard captain, lynched during the Porteous Riots in 1736

Sir Charles Tupper, sixth Prime Minister of Canada

Charles Umpherston Aitchison, Lieutenant-Governor of the Punjab

John Witherspoon, only cleric to sign the American Declaration of Independence, and president of Princeton University

Ewen Bremner, actor (*Trainspotting*, *Black Hawk Down*)

Ken Stott, actor (Inspector Rebus)

Sean Connery, actor (James Bond)

Ronnie Corbett, comedian and actor (*The Two Ronnies*)

And finally:
David Morris, world champion pie-eater

City of Books

Books are hard to avoid in Edinburgh. Apart from being the world's first UNESCO City of Literature and the incredible number of fictional detectives who roam the city on the page, there are dozens of bookshops. A stroll up the West Port will reveal some treasures.

Jim Haynes, who later co-invented The Traverse Theatre, opened Britain's first ever Paperback Book Shop in George Square.

The precursor of the Book Festival was an exercise in 1983 when, to save money, the writers who came were billeted on local literary, arts and music folk. As Ione said, 'Some poor bugger got allocated William Burroughs!'

The West Port BookFest is a 'distributed' event around various cramped, atmospheric book shops in August each year.

Fictional Detectives

Apart from Inspector Rebus, Edinburgh is home to many fictional detectives, including:

James M'Levy, who wasn't fictional, but who wrote fictionalised accounts of his own exploits as Chief of Detectives in the 1860s.

Chief Superintendant Bob Skinner, created by Quintin Jardine as 'Britain's toughest cop'.

Quintilian Dalrymple, Paul Johnston's private eye in a dystopian near-future Edinburgh.

Jack Parlabane, in Christopher Brookmyre's hilarious but serious-satirical crime novels.

Jim Meldrum, Frederic Lindsay's middle-aged, grumpy, psychological Detective Inspector.

Dr Steven Dunbar in Ken McClure's medical chiller/thrillers, firmly based on his real-life science research job.

Isabel Dalhousie, Alexander McCall Smith's posh and prissy Edinburgh equivalent to Mma Ramotswe.

Joyce Holms' **Fizz and Buchanan**, a pairing of a boring lawyer and his sparky young assistant.

Alanna Knight's creations, the Victorian Detective **Inspector Faro** and his enquiring daughter, **Rose McQuinn**.

Performing Arts Organisations

National
Scottish Chamber Orchestra
Edinburgh Quartet, a professional string quartet
Youth, School and University
Edinburgh Youth Orchestra
Scottish Schools Orchestra Trust
Edinburgh University String Orchestra
Edinburgh University Sinfonia
Edinburgh University Symphony Orchestra
Edinburgh University Chamber Orchestra

Amateur and Community
Colinton Orchestra
Edinburgh Orchestral Ensemble
Edinburgh Symphony Orchestra
Meadows Chamber Orchestra
New Edinburgh Orchestra
The Open Orchestra
Phoenix Wind Band
The Really Terrible Orchestra

Theatre Companies
Bedlam Theatre, home to the Edinburgh University Theatre
Co. (EUTC), housed in the former New North Free Church
Festival Theatre
King's Theatre
Edinburgh Playhouse
Queen's Hall, which stages classical, jazz, blues, pop, rock,
world, folk and comedy, and is home to the Scottish Chamber
Orchestra
Royal Lyceum

Edinburgh's iconic **Traverse Theatre** had an unlikely beginning in 1963, and a mistaken name.

It began as theatre club in James Court, Lawnmarket, which had been a flop-house and a brothel known variously as 'Hell's Kitchen' and 'Kelly's Paradise'. The idea, as envisioned by founders Jim Haynes, John Calder and art impressario and all-round Edinburgh legend Richard Demarco, was to keep the idea of the Edinburgh Festival going all year. It is still called 'the Fringe that Escaped' in some quarters. Some sixty seats were rescued form the Palace Cinema and arranged either side of the stage in the long, narrow and low-ceilinged room. Terry Lane, the first director, thought this set-up was called 'traverse' (it's actually 'transverse').

A Theatre Conference in its first year involving Jim Haynes and Kenneth Tynan, and a 'Happening' (if that's the word) organised by American performance art pioneer Allan Kaprow established its notoriety and experimental bent. At only the second performance, actress Colette O'Neill was accidentally stabbed by a real knife used, as Richard Demarco says, because they couldn't afford a fake one. The Edinburgh police helped with publicity by constantly threatrening to raid it because of the 'obscene' performances and homosexual activity. There was also exhibition space there until 1966 when the Richard Demarco Gallery was established elsewhere.

The James Court site was essentially condemned and in 1969 the Traverse moved to a loft in the West Bow, at the east end of the Grassmarket, with 100 'seats' more flexibly arranged.

In 1992, the Traverse became a £3.3 million purpose-built two theatres and café-bar in the Saltire Court development on Cambridge Street/Castle Terrace. It is renowned for fostering leading-edge new writing and youth theatre, and is the leading light in the Edinburgh arts landscape.

Film

Edinburgh has its own Film Commission, Edinburgh Film Focus, to help with productions and locations in the city, the Lothians and the Borders.

Burke and Hare
There have been any number of depictions of the dastardly pair and their Edinburgh hunting-grounds, most recently the 2010 extravaganza from John Landis, starring Simon Pegg and Andy (Gollum) Serkis.

Chariots of Fire
Much of this 1981 film centres on Eric Liddel, and the Edinburgh skyline is a backdrop.

Harry Potter
Fettes College was an inspiration for Hogwart's.

Hallam Foe
David Mackenzie's rather strange 2007 study of obsession has the anti-hero perched in the clocktower of the Balmoral Hotel, spying on others.

One Day
Lone Scherfig's 2011 adaptation of David Nicholls' romantic novel starts and finishes in Edinburgh, notably Old College quadrangle and Cockburn Street.

The Prime of Miss Jean Brodie
Muriel Spark drew on her own time at Gillespie's school for her 1961 novella, filmed in 1969.

Shallow Grave
Danny Boyle's 1994 black comedy – starring then-unknowns Ewan McGregor and Christopher Eccleston alongside old-stagers Peter Mullan and Ken (Rebus) Stott – was set in Edinburgh but mainly shot in Glasgow (apart from the necessary New Town interiors).

Trainspotting
Likewise, director Boyle largely filmed Irvine Welsh's Edinburgh-set novel in Glasgow. The title refers to drug-taking in the disused Leith railway station.

Business Then

Edinburgh was famous for books, brewing and banking – but there were other trades and industries. In the 1880s, Francis Groome's Ordnance Gazetteer of Scotland said:

'Her manufactures, perhaps, are more diversified, exhibit a larger aggregate of genius, than those of many other great towns'.

Linen manufacture sank into decline, as did weaving in imitation of Indian shawls and what became known as Paisley patterns. Silk manufacture, started in 1841, was also not a success. But the Fountainbridge building was turned over to manufacture of india-rubber overshoes in 1855 and vulcanite production started in 1862.

Other big industries were carpet-making, coach-building, glass-making, type-founding and various kinds of jewellery. Paper mills in the North Esk valley supplied the wholesale stationers. But brewing and distilling had long been a staple, along with flour-milling. The fine arts were also a major trade, especially painters and sculptors.

The arrival of the railways and the Union Canal connected Edinburgh with the mines of Midlothian and Stirlingshire and, via Leith and Granton, to the commercial ports of the whole of Britain and the Continent.

The other major business was that of law and government, and the various finance and broking houses.

But Edinburgh was possibly most famous for printing, publishing and literature, employing thousands in the manufacturing aspects over and above the creative spirits who produced the works. The first printing press was set up in the Cowgate less than 30 years after Caxton started his press in Westminster. Allan Ramsay published and sold his own songs and had a circulating library. Constable first published Scott's *Waverley* novels and the *Edinburgh Review*, and later came famous names like Blackwood, Black, Tait's *Edinburgh Magazine* and the brothers William and Robert Chambers who produced the *Encyclopedia Britannica* (1771) and much more. Edinburgh was not only a centre for literature, but also what we would now call standard reference non-fiction. John Ged invented stereotyping, Nelson's used the advances in engraving and lithography for their famous maps, and bookbinding was a major trade in its own right.

Business Now

Today, the major non-public sector employers are in banking, insurance and finance generally. Edinburgh is the second biggest financial centre in the UK after the City of London, and fourth in Europe.

The Bank of Scotland, Clydesdale Bank, HSBC, Lloyds, JP Morgan, Royal Bank of Scotland, Standard Life, Scottish Widows, Tesco Bank, Virgin Money, and others are headquartered in or near the city, many in the new Exchange District. Some are at the purpose-built Edinburgh Park, near the airport, alongside major international concerns like BT, Diageo, Fujitsu and Telewest.

Brewing is not so prominent as it once was, especially since the closure of Scottish & Newcastle's Fountain brewery in 2005 – which first opened as McEwan's in 1856 – left Caledonian as the largest brewer in the city.

Edinburgh still punches above its weight in publishing though, with major firms like Birlinn/Polygon, Black & White, Canongate, Chambers Harrap, Edinburgh University Press and Mainstream – joined by Dunedin Academic Press, Floris, Luath and other independents.

Freedom of the City

The Freedom of the City is the greatest tribute Edinburgh can offer any person and is conferred by the Lord Provost to persons 'who have distinguished themselves through their work or efforts, or to recognise the respect and high esteem in which they are held by the people of the City of Edinburgh'. It is a civic honour and as such confers no special rights or privileges.

Historically, Freemen and Burgesses have the same rights and privileges, with full rights to trade within the Burgh, specifically on market days. It has been bestowed on (among others):

Field-Marshal Bernard Montgomery (1946)

General Dwight David Eisenhower (1946)

HRH Princess Elizabeth (1947)

HRH Prince Philip, Duke of Edinburgh (1949)

Sir Donald Charles Cameron, Mayor of Dunedin (1949)

Rt Hon. Earl Mountbatten of Burma and the **Countess Mountbatten of Burma** (1954)

HM King Olav V of Norway (1962)

Yehudi Menuhin (1965)

Sir Alex Douglas-Home (1969)

Sean Connery (1991)

Nelson Mandela (1997)

Aung San Suu Kyi (in absentia, 2005)

Fictional Characters

Everyone knows about Deacon Brodie, Jekyll and Hyde, Ian Rankin's Inspector Rebus and Muriel Stark's Miss Jean Brodie, but how about:

Prince Edmund Plantagenet Blackadder, who was Duke of Edinburgh in the first series.

Dr Fu Manchu, Sax Rohmer's oriental criminal mastermind, who studied at Edinburgh.

Harry Potter, whose earlier books were written by J.K. Rowling in various Edinburgh cafés.

Toad of Toad Hall, conceived by Edinburgh-born Kenneth Grahame as bedtime stories for his son, Alastair.

James Bond, educated at Fettes College, according to creator Ian Fleming, after expulsion from Eton for seducing a maid.

Long John Silver, created in *Treasure Island* by Robert Louis Stevenson (along with many staples of the genre such as swashbuckling, one-legged pirates, treasure marked with an 'X', and parrots who say 'pieces of eight').

Mrs Doubtfire, not so much created by novelist Anne Fine as half-remembered from the real-life clay-pipe-smoking owner of a bric-a-brac shop in Stockbridge by that name.

Shrek – why else did Mike Myers give him an Edinburgh accent?

Civil War Memorial

The only statue of Abraham Lincoln in Scotland, and the only monument to the American Civil War outside the USA, is in Old Calton Cemetary, a two-minute walk from Waverly Station. It commemorates the Scots who fought in the Civil War and came about because Margaret, wife of Sgt Major MacEwan, wasn't awarded a pension. The American Consul in Edinburgh at the time – who gloried in the overly Scottish name of Wallace Bruce – took up her case. Not only did she get her pension, he persuaded Rockefeller, JP morgan, Carnegie and others to contribute to the memorial. It was unveiled on 21 August 1893, and John McEwan was the first name engraved on it. Another soldier, William Duff, is actually buried beneath and the rest are buried nearby.

Wallace Bruce wrote a poem to be read at the unveiling, but the weather was typically Scottish and terrible, so the ceremony was cut short and the poem never got read. And not long after Margaret was awarded the pension, the US government changed the law so that to draw a pension you had to live there... so she upped sticks and left for Chicago with her children.

And Finally...

How many railway stations does Edinburgh have?
The standard answer is 'two', but as it happens:

Brunstane

Curriehill

Dalmeny

Edinburgh Park

Edinburgh Waverley

Haymarket

Kingsknowe

Newcraighall

Shawfair (planned)

Slateford

South Gyle

Wester Hailes

Edinburgh Airport Rail Link was cancelled.

Strangely, Brunstane and Newcraighall are on the Fife Circle, handy if you want to visit your Mum in Kirkcaldy.

Picture Credits

Unless otherwise stated, pictures are either by Carolyn Becket or Bruce Durie, or not in need of a credit.

Page:

3. Coat of arms.

7. Hollar's 1670 map of Edinburgh

9. The Grassmarket, looking east (top) and west (bottom)

13. Nova Scotia plaque at Edinburgh Castle

15. The crag-and-tail of Castle Hill meant that tenements stretched down the back, as here in Victoria Street

21. Statue of David, Florence (Sergi Montaner)

23. The ethnic mix of Edinburgh's streets

25. Calton Hill, with the Nelson Monument and 'Edinburgh's Disgrace', overshadowing the old St Andrew's House; the ball on the cross is raised and drops every day when the 1 p.m. gun fires, as a visual time-signal to ships in the Forth

27. The old North British Hotel at North Bridge, now The Balmoral, was the railway hotel for Waverley Station. The clock is, by tradition, always three minutes fast, to encourage travellers not to miss their trains

29. Looking up the Royal Mile to St Giles

30-41. Princes Street to Calton Hill; Holyrood Palace; Princes Street Gardens; Calton Jail (long gone); Grassmarket and Castle; so-called John Knox House; Gret Hall at the Castle; Scott Monument; Mercat Cross; Mary, Queen of Scots; Holyrood Abbey; Forth Bridge

43. Craigmillar Castle

49. MacKenzie's tomb at Greyfriars

53. Cannongate Tolbooth; Zara Philips and Mike Tindall were married in Canongate Kirk in 2011

55. Fossilisec tree, the Botanics; Hermitage of Braid; Sandy Bell's Tavern

57. Sure, it's a cliché, but everyone wants a photo with 'the dug'. Or, go for a walk with poet Robert Fergusson

58. Edinburgh has its share of high-rises as well as medieval garrets, Victorian tenements and Georgian townhouses, but the views are still unbeatable

71. Writer's Museum at Lady Stair's House

73. Holyrood today

75. Dynamic Earth

77. Scott Monument

78. Edinburgh is full of architectural surprises. These pillars, taken from Argyle House, Portobello, are made from Coade Stone

79. Farmers' Market; West End church; that's not a cat, it's a gargoyle that has lost its wings

81. When looking at buildings, don't miss the heraldic details on many of them; Cordiners, the Scottish National Portrait Gallery

83. Walter Scott (courtesy of the Library of Congress, LC-DIG-ppmsc-07693)

87. Joppa Beach

91. Napier University;

93. Did RLS base his map of Treasure island on Princes Street gardens which he often visited when he was a boy? Go there and judge for yourself!

95. Tony Blair went there for real, but fictionally so did James Bond, and it was one of the inspirations for Harry Potter's Hogwart's

97. Len Partridge

99. Edinburgh New Town, designed by James Craig

111. Picture courtesy of and © Peter Stubbs, peter.stubbs@edinphoto.org. uk. Yes, it's a Tardis! This police box is still on the corner of Drummond Street and The Pleasance

119. A typical Waverley illustration

123. General Dwight D. Eisenhower, Supreme Allied Commander, talks with Major Gen. Matthew B. Ridgway, CG, 18th Corps, at a headquarters in Germany, during General Eisenhower's tour of the western front (courtesy of the Library of Congress, LC-DIG-ppmsca-19037)